REMEMBRANCE OF GOD'S DIVINE WORD

31 Day Devotional for Women

RHONDA WIGGINS

Remembrance of God's Divine Word
Daily Inspiration for Women
Through God's Word and Songs

CONTENTS

DEDICATION

This Devotional is dedicated in honor of my grandmother, Birdie Mae Wilson Johnson, whom we affectionately called Mama Birdie.

Mama Birdie always had a sweet spirit, she always cared about everyone. She would put everyone before her needs to help and make sure her family was alright. My grandmother touched so many lives in her lifetime. She was a beautiful and loving God-fearing woman who had a heart of gold. My sisters and I are blessed to be raised by two loving grandparents, Conrad O. Johnson Sr. and Birdie Johnson. God had the perfect plan by placing us in Grandma's care. There was so much peace and love in our home. My grandmother ministered to everyone by praying, reading her daily devotion, or singing and playing her organ. She instilled in me so many values of life. I remember as a young girl sitting on the floor with my sisters and cousins, we would watch and listen to her play the organ while singing her favorite songs. Among those songs include:

- How Great Thou Art
- His Eyes is on the Sparrow
- It is Well with my Soul
- Blessed Assurance
- You can't beat God's Giving
- Great Is Thy Faith-fullness
- Oh I Need Thee Every Hour
- Remember Only What You Do for Christ will Last

There are so many other Inspirational songs.

I pray that this Devotional will help to touch someone's life and receive the encouraging words that God has put in my heart. This Devotional is based on the songs and God's word through Scriptures that have ministered to me throughout my life. I believe God wants me to continue to be that beacon of light and carry the torch to minister and be a blessing to children, young ladies, and seniors. I also believe God wants me to embrace those that need the embracing of God's love as my beautiful grandmother, Birdie Mae Wilson Johnson did.

To all Grandmothers that have gone to be with the Lord, thank you for instilling God's love and His word. And to the Grandmothers who are still serving the Lord, keep instilling God's Divine Word in your grandchildren. Continue to Pray and Praise God. Give Him the Glory in Everything. Hallelujah!

Much Love
Music Encourages the Soul
Meditation of the Mind
Communication to the Heart

ACKNOWLEGEMENT

I would like to thank my husband for his love, support, and encouragement. I'll also like to thank my parents for their unconditional love and support; and my daughter Jessica, saying, "mama, you can do this?" I'm so proud of you, and my Auntie for her prayers. It's a blessing to have a family that shows love, and respect for one another and supports each other. Count your Blessings, and don't forget to tell your loved ones that you love them.

1

Song: Great Is Thy Faithfulness
Topic: New Mercies I See
Scripture: Lamentations 3:22-23 CSB

Because of the Lord's Faithful love we do not perish, for all His mercies never end. They are new every morning; great is your faithfulness!

We are blessed, each morning with God's Grace and Mercies. Morning by morning, new mercies I see. Great is Thy Faithfulness, Lord unto me. When you have hope in God, you are waiting with confident expectations that He will deliver you from unforeseen circumstances. We don't know what tomorrow may bring but, we have hope and trust in Him. We don't deserve Grace, it is a gift from God; an unmerited favor from Him. He is faithful and just to all mankind. God gives us opportunities every morning when He wakes us up to discover and experience more of His love. God is faithful, He keeps His promises of protecting and providing for us each day. My God is a merciful God and full of Grace.

God The Father showed mercy on us when He sacrificed His Son, Christ Jesus, on the cross to pay the price for our sins. Yes, God's mercy and forgiveness are real, it is a gift to the confessing sinner. He forgives you of your sins and shows you kindness and compassion. Psalm 51:1-2 Lord, Great is Thy Faithfulness. New Mercies I see. You give me strength each day and hope for tomorrow. Great is Thy Faithfulness, Morning by morning, new mercies I see.

Spiritual Food for Thought: Remember God's new Mercies every day.

Scripture References

Hope – Romans 5:2-4, Isaiah 40:31, Psalm 130:5
Grace- Ephesians 2:8-9, 2nd Corinthians 12:9, 2nd Timothy 2:1
Mercy- Lamentations 3:22-23, Matthew 5:7, Luke 6:36

D A Y

2

Song: How Great Thou Art
Topic: Faithfulness of God's Love
Scripture: Psalm 92:5 NKJV

O Lord, how great are your works! Your thoughts are very deep.

As I was looking through my journals, I saw a message on September 1, 2017, where the Holy Spirit put in my heart this song, *How Great Thou Art*. And today, May 25, 2020, I'm writing about this same song in my Devotional. When I hear this song, it reminds me of the Greatness of God in all of His Divine Works. This song also reminds me of my friend, Hanq Neal. He sang this song around the world with his anointed voice; the love and adoration he had for God could be felt. God, You are Alpha and Omega, the Beginning and the End. The words to this song are so powerful; it starts off with *Oh Lord my God*. When I'm in awesome wonder, considered all the worlds Thy hands have made. You created this vast universe with just a thought. And then it ends with adoration, *how great Thou art, how great Thou art.* Knowing the goodness of God, we should give Him the Highest Praise. When we are worshipping God and showing our love for Him we are giving respect and reverence to our mighty God.

Spiritual Food for Thought: Knowing the goodness of God gives us an opportunity to show adoration for Him. We should Praise God for all of the marvelous works that He has done. And the Highest Praise is Hallelujah. This is an expression of rejoicing.

Scripture References

Holy Spirit- Ephesians 1:13-14, Romans 8:2-6, John 14:26
Divine- 2nd Peter 1:3-4, 2nd Peter 1:4, Romans 1:20
Praise- Psalm 150:6, Psalm 63:1-4, Psalm 9:1

D A Y

3

Song: Precious Lord Take My Hand
Topic: God's Pure Knowledge of Man
Scripture: Psalm 139:10 NKJV

Even there your hand shall lead me, and your right hand shall hold me.

When you feel destitute, you can't see because you are in so much darkness in the storms of life and you don't know what to do. Turn to God our Heavenly Father, He will not disappoint you. As the late Thomas A. Dorsey, one of the most influential Christian songwriters wrote, Precious Lord, Take My hand, lead me on, let me stand, I am tired, I am weak, I am worn; through the storm, through the night, lead me on to the light. Take my hand precious Lord, lead me home. When you ask God to strengthen you through tough times by taking your hand, to lead, guide, and help you, you're putting total trust in Him. And when you asked God to let you stand, you are asking Him to strengthen you through difficult times. Remember in His word, He promised that

He will never leave you nor forsake you (Hebrews 13:5). God also said in Matthew 28:20, I will be with you always, even to the end of the age. He hears your cries and prayers and keeps His promises. God will bring you through the darkness to the marvelous light. You have to Yield to the Spirit of God. Continue to hold on to God's unchanging hand. He is the same as yesterday to today and forever. He never changes.

Spiritual food for thought: Once we have gone through darkness and come to the light. We have to remember God's Promises by taking a stand to witness and share with others what God has done for us.

Scripture References

Yield- 2nd Chronicles 30:8, Romans 6:13-14
Obedient- James1:22, Isaiah 1:19, Deuteronomy 5:33
Promises- Isaiah 40:31, Isaiah 43:2, Matthew 7:7

D A Y

4

Song: It Is Well With My Soul
Topic: The Gift of Peace
Scripture: John 14:27 CSB

Peace I leave with you. My peace I give to you. I do not give to you as the world gives. Don't let your heart be troubled or fearful.

Regardless of our Season in Life. God teaches us to find and accept internal peace through Him. God is not promising the absence of storms. But He gives us perfect peace in the midst of a storm. When our minds or our Faith starts to waver and focus on the storm, we are not putting our trust in God, we are focusing on the circumstances. God wants us to focus totally on Him. And by doing that, we need to study God's Word and know the scriptures so that when Satan tries to attack us Spiritually, Mentally, Physically, and Emotionally we will put God's word to action by standing on the promises of God through His Divine Word with prayer and gratitude. As we walk in the Spirit of God we are being obedient and totally depend on God. You will experience calmness in the midst of the storm. Maybe your storm is not over, but you know that God heard your prayer and that's when you receive the peace in your heart. In Philippians 4:6-7 it says, and the peace of God, which surpasses all understanding will guard your hearts and minds in Christ Jesus. The Bible is your Sword.

Spiritual food for thought: So what are you going to do today? Will you receive the internal peace that God will bless you with therefore letting the peace of Christ rule in your hearts?

Scripture References

Peace- John 14:27, Phillippians 4:7-8, Numbers 6:24-26
Prayer- Mark 11:24, 1ˢᵗ Thessalonians 5:16-18, 1ˢᵗ John 5:14
Word of God- Hebrews 4-12, Psalm 119:105, James 1:22

D A Y

5

Song: I Surrender All
Topic: Reconciliation with God
Scripture: 2 Corinthians 5:17-18 NKJV

Therefore, if anyone is in Christ, he is a new creation old things have passed away; behold all things have become new. Now all things are of God, who has reconciled us to Himself through Jesus Christ, and has given us the ministry of reconciliation.

When you are tired of the way you are living and your thoughts are not aligned up with God's way, that's when you surrender all to God. When you have a change of heart you will begin to have a personal relationship with God. Let go and allow your all to the will and teachings of God. We all have sinned and fallen short of the Glory of God. God is in charge anyway, so when you surrender, you give up on the things that were not of God. As believers' life starts to change, we are transformed into the likeness and renewal of Christ. The old has passed away, Therefore you are called to live in accordance with your new self or identity. Instead of us living for ourselves, we start living for Christ. We begin to walk in the light that reflects from God to be able to witness to others that are lost in this sinful world. We as believers of Christ have the duty to tell others that they can be reconciled to Him as well. We need to let God take control and put it all in His hands. Because we can't do anything without God.

Spiritual food for thought: Will you continue to live in this sin-sick world or Will you surrender all and live for Christ?

Scripture References

Reconciliation- Romans 5:8, Ephesians 4:32, 2nd Corinthians 5:19
Surrender- Romans 12:2, James 4:7,
Sin- 1st John 1:19, Romans 3:23-24, Psalm 51:1-2

D A Y

6

Song: On Christ the Solid Rock
Topic: Two Foundations
Scripture: Matthew 7:24-26 CSB

Therefore, everyone who hears these words of mine and acts on them will be like a wise man who built his house on the rock. The rain fell, the rivers rose, and the winds blew and pounded that house. Yet it didn't collapse, because its foundation was on the rock.

To have a Sturdy Foundation you have to have the wisdom and knowledge of God and be able to apply the word of God. But if you don't adhere to God's word, you will be on shaky ground, when unforeseen circumstances and storms come your way you will get overwhelmed and won't focus on God's word rather you will start focusing on the situation that you don't have any control over. But, I do know who has total control over every situation or storm that comes our way and that is Jesus, my Lord, and Savior. You have to have the Assurance, that certainty, and self-confidence in your Faith in God. The foundation of Christ is God and His Word. Because all Scripture is God-breathed. You must build a strong Foundation by feeding your Spirit the Word of God. Without that foundation, we are not able to grow in our faith daily. Christ Himself, remains our Rock, our fortress, our deliverer our source of security, and the unshakable foundation for our lives. Psalms 18:2 says, God, you are my strength, in whom I will trust; my shield and the horn of my salvation, my stronghold. The horn symbolizes strength.

Spiritual Food for Thought: God's word is the core of our foundation. His word is the solid foundation for us to stand on. Stand on the sure foundation of Christ and not shaky grounds. That Rock is Jesus the only one I know.

Scripture References

Rock- 1st Samuel 2:2, Psalm 71:3, Matthew 16:18
Foundation- 2nd Timothy 2:19, Proverbs 10:25
Jesus- Hebrews 12:2, John11:40, 1st John 4:15

D A Y

7

Song: Break Every Chain
Topic: Grateful to the Lord for His Great Works of Deliverance

Scripture: Psalms107:14-15 NKJV

He brought them out of darkness and the shadow of death, and broke the chains in pieces. Oh, that men would give thanks to the Lord for His goodness, And for His Wonderful works to the children of men!

We have so many strongholds in our lives. It may be in our relationships, addiction, emotions, finances, or mental health. As Christians, we are given power, strength, and faith. When we call upon the Lord to deliver us from Spiritual attacks and Satan's schemes we have to have Faith. If we have faith and do not practice the faith, that is disobedience. We have to be Obedient in our Faith. That is to know God, trust God, and know He will be with you. If or when we cry out to God He hears our cries and prayers. Be sincere in asking God for Deliverance, He will help you. God will never leave you nor forsake you, He supplies all the needs of His people. Whatever your need, be it the Deliverance from any stronghold of darkness, remember that God will bring you out of the pit of darkness and into the light, if you submit to Him. We as Christians are to be receptive to God, fulfilling our highest destiny in choosing to obey the Lord in the matter of submission. This does not make us inferior as a person when we submit to God, for we remain children of God and we are greatly accepted and loved by the Lord.

Spiritual food for thought: You have to be prepared to receive the Deliverance that God has for you.

Scripture References

Deliverance- Psalm 34:4, 2nd Samuel 22-2, Psalm 34:17
Strongholds- Psalms 18:2, 2nd Samuel 22:3, 2nd Corinthians 10:3-4
Submission-James 4:7, Romans 8:7, Jeremiah 17:10

D A Y

8

Song: Yes God is Real
Topic: Ever Present of God
Scripture: Psalms139:1-4 CSB

Lord you have searched me and known me. You know when I sit down and when I stand up; you understand my thoughts from far away. You observe my travels and my rest; you are aware of all my ways. Before a word is on my tongue, you know all about it Lord.

Yes! God is Real I feel Him in my soul, for He has washed and made me whole. I love to hear my Pastor sing this song, and his father sings this song also. How do you know He's real? Because you can feel His Holy Power, His love for me is like pure gold. God is omniscient (all-knowing). Psalms 139:4 says, "before a word is on my tongue, you know all about it Lord." GOD knows everything, including the past, present, and future, He isn't surprised about anything, nothing is new to Him. There is nothing you can hide from God. God knows our desires, motives, and words before we even speak them.

He even knows the thoughts and intents of our hearts. He is Almighty through His infinite Wisdom. God is omnipotent (all-powerful). John 1:3 says, "All things were made through Him." In Genesis Chapter 1:1-5, "God created the heavens and the earth. Then it was darkness and God said let there be light." God is not limited to physical limitations like a man is. God has power over the whole Universe. God has power over the wind and water. In Psalms 107:25, He spoke and raised a stormy wind and stirred up the waves of the sea. He causes His wind to blow and the waters flow. He has all power in His hands. I remember as a child we use to sing a song that says that God has the whole world in His hand. God is omnipresent (all present). Psalm 139:7-12 says, "where can I go from your Spirit? Or where can I flee from your presence?" David His servant tried to flee from His presence, but could not. He's present everywhere we can't hide from Him. God is present in every situation. He's present in the midst of our storms and tribulations. God knows all about your troubles and the benefits of experiencing Him are infinite.

Spiritual Food for Thought: If you have any doubt about knowing that God is real. Just think about this, who wakes you up every morning, who protects you every day, and who provides for your every need?

Scripture References

God – Isaiah 40:28-29, Joshua 1:9, Isaiah 25:1
Omniscient- 1ˢᵗ John 3:20, Psalm 139-4, Isiah 46:9-10
Omnipotent- Jeremiah 32:17&27, Ephesians 1:19, Matthew 19:26
Omnipresent- Psalms 139:7-12, Matthew 18:20, Jeremiah 23:23-24

D A Y

9

Song: Every Praise
Topic: The Contentment of Those Who Trust in God
Scripture: Psalm34:1 NKJV

I will bless the Lord at all times; His praise shall continually be in my mouth.

God, I give You all the Praises. I can't thank You enough, You are my Savior, healer and my deliverer, yes You are. When you think of the goodness of God, and how He delivered you from certain situations that have occurred in your life, you will discover that God deserves the Praise. When God healed you when the doctors said it was nothing else they could do, God deserves the Praise. When you didn't know if you were going to have food to feed your family, money to pay bills, or even shelter, God made a way out of no way, He's a way-maker and He deserves the Praise. In Praising God we should Praise God all day long. If a situation looks dim or cloudy, we should still give God every Praise. God knows the outcome of every situation or storm that we encounter, He just wants us to Trust, Praise, and honor Him. When we get in difficult times we need to continue to Praise God, not just when things are going smooth. Just be still and watch how God works your situations out. Be thankful in all circumstances. 1st Thessalonians 5:16-18 NKJV says, "rejoice always, pray without ceasing, in everything give thanks; for this is the will of God in Christ Jesus for you." And as we continue to Praise Him, God receives the Glory.

Spiritual Food For Thought: Think about the goodness of God. And remember to give Him every Praise.

Scripture References

Praises – Psalm 47:6, Hebrews 13:15, Psalm 28:7
Honor- Psalm 32:8, Revelation 5:13, 2nd Peter 1:17
Way-maker- Matthew 19:26, Hebrews 10:23, Isaiah 35:6

D A Y

10

Song: I Want to Say Thank You
Topic: Joy in Gods Mercies
Scripture: Psalm 106:1 NKJV

Praise the Lord!

Oh give thanks to the Lord, for He is good! For His mercy endures forever.

Every day is a day of Thanksgiving. Worship and Praise Him in Adoration. We have so many things to thank God for. When I think of all His Goodness and all the things He's done for me, I can't thank Him enough. We are to be internally grateful even when things are not going right or the way we think things should go. We as Christians or Believers of Christ should exalt God's name continually, for His mercies endures forever. Not just what He has done for you and me but, because of who He is. God is Elohim, the creator of heaven and earth, who was the beginning. God is Jehovah-Jireh, our provider, who sees all of our needs and provides for us. God is Jehovah-Rapha, our healer, the one who makes bitter experiences sweet. You heard my prayers and forgave all of my sins You saved, delivered, and healed me even when I didn't deserve it. In your word, you said Your Grace is sufficient and Your Mercies are everlasting. God is Jehovah-Nissi, my Banner, my Victory, my protector, my shield, my keeper, my hiding place, and my shelter. When you need direction in your life, let go and let God navigate you, He will never guide you the wrong way. He is Jehovah- Rohi, my Shepherd, I lack nothing. Remember to give thanks in everything in spite of what your circumstances may be.

Spiritual Food for Thought: Remember to Thank God every day!

Scripture References

Adoration – Isaiah 6:3, Deuteronomy 6:5, Joshua 22:5
Christians- Galatians 5:25, 1st Thessalonians 4:1, Matthew 5:16
Thanksgiving- Psalm 136, 1st Thessalonians 5:16-18, Colossians 2:6-7

D A Y

11

Song: You Know my Name
Topic: Assurance of Abiding in the Presence of God
Scripture: Psalm 91:14 NKJV

Because he has set his love upon me therefore I will deliver him; I will set him on high, because he has known my name.

Lord, You know my name. Oh how you walk with me and talk to me and you tell me I'm your own. God, you are a comforter when I need comfort, sometimes He comforts us directly, sometimes through circumstances, and sometimes through the people He places in our lives. You counsel me and Your counsel is sure through Your guidance and direction of life. Psalm 16:7 says, "I will bless the Lord who counsels me; my heart also instructs me in the night seasons." Lord I know you are with me and I know I'm your own. God is love, you are exactly who God intended you to be. We are all God's children who are uniquely, intricately, precisely, and wonderfully created in His own image. God knows all about us. Remember you are one of a kind creation for which there is no comparison. He created you for His own purpose so that you might reflect a unique aspect of His Glory. God reveals Himself to all creation, and He greatly desires to have a relationship with you. God created you to be a Godly woman, spirit-filled, joyous, kindhearted, who loves Jesus, yourself, and your family. Yes, Jesus walks with you and talks with you and tells you that you are His own. God, please let me hold on to Your unchanging hands as You continue to walk and talk to me.

Spiritual Food for Thought: Remember God knows your name.

Scripture References

Comforter- 2nd Corinthians 1:3-4, Psalm 23:4, Matthew 11:28
Counsel- Psalm32:8, Proverbs 28:26
Trust- 1st John 5:14, Psalm 27:14, Proverbs 3:5-6
Image- 2nd Corinthians 3:18, Genesis 1:27, Romans 8:29

D A Y

12

Song: Be Encourage
Topic: God will always send an Encourager
Scripture: Deuteronomy 31:8 NKJV

And the Lord, He is the one who goes before you. He will be with you, He will not leave you nor forsake you; do not fear nor be dismayed.

Deuteronomy 31:7-8 (NKJV), "Then Moses called Joshua and said to him be strong and of good courage." We as Christians are to encourage one another. Speak words of blessings. We don't know what a person is going through, we as humans usually allow our flesh to get discouraged over certain circumstances. God places people in our lives for a reason and season. My mom encourages and ministers to so many people at her job. She would always tell one young man to pull up his pants and then she will go ahead to give him encouraging words because she saw that he needed some guidance. My mom would witness to him about God. He told my mom he had been reading his grandmother's bible and it was falling apart, so my mom bought him one. He started asking more questions about God and my mom invited him to church. As my mom continued witnessing and encouraging him, he started having hope. He joined the church and accepted Christ as His Lord and Savior and was baptized. You never know whose lives you have touched by giving encouragement or just being a listening ear. In 1st Thessalonians, it says, "therefore encourage one another and build each other up as you are already doing." Use the gift of encouragement that God has blessed you with to bless someone else. As you encourage someone, pray for them, and let them know that you are praying for them. Sometimes we don't know how meaningful that is.

Spiritual Food for Thought: God bless me to encourage someone today. To be the light that reflects from you.

Scripture References

Encouragement- Hebrews 10:24-25, Psalm 27:1,
1st Thessalonians 5:11
Witness-Mark 16:15-16, Romans 10:15, John 12:32
Baptism-Acts 2:38, John 3:5, 1st Corinthians 12:13
Testimony- Mark 5:19, Psalm 22:22, 1st John 5:10-11

D A Y

13

Song: It's A Mighty Good Day to Praise the Lord!
Topic: Sacrifices of Praises to God
Scripture: Hebrews13:15 AMP

Through Him, therefore, let us at all times offer up to God a Sacrifice of Praise, which is the fruit of lips that thankfully acknowledge and confess and Glorify His Name.

When I think of God's goodness of waking me up each day with health, strength, and a sound mind, It's a mighty good Day to Praise the Lord. When you think of all the provision and protection that the Lord has blessed you with, it's a mighty good day to Praise the Lord. In the midst of it all, the corruption, confusion, and darkness of this world, It's still a mighty good day to Praise the Lord. We have to remember who God is. God is everything. He's Alpha and Omega the beginning and the end. He is our bright morning star. When we offer sacrifices of Praise to our Lord Jesus Christ. It is by Him, in Him, with Him, to Him, and for Him. Our Praise will never cease when we keep our focus on Him. Job 11:13

says, "if you prepare your heart, and stretch out your hands toward Him," this is a form of a posture of prayer as well as of praise.

Spiritual Food for Thought: Remembering to Praise the Lord each day. Don't let obstacles, distractions, or the business of the day stop you from praising the Lord.

Scripture References

Sacrifices- Hebrew 13:15, Jonah 2:9, Psalm 119:105
Praise- Psalm 30:12, Psalm 6:-20, Isaiah 25:1
Alpha and Omega- Revelation 22:13, Isaiah 44:6, Revelation 1:8

14

Song: Order My Steps
Topic: Encouragement of Godly Living
Scripture: Proverbs 16:9 NKJV

A person's heart plans his way, but the Lord determines his steps.

When you have a detour in life, it could be various detours, it could be financial, Physical, or Spiritual. God wants us to trust Him. Proverbs 3:5-6 says, "Trust in the Lord with all your heart, and lean not on your own understanding; in all your ways acknowledge Him; and He shall direct your paths." You are so important to God. Just trust Him for guidance and His promises and think of His goodness. As God is ordering your steps and as He is leading you through this detour, you have to be willing and obedient. The road or your steps might be bumpy, But, God will smoothen the path and make it straight. Trusting God is a conscious dependence upon Him. You have to speak God's word into your situation or problem as He is ordering your steps. Then, when you are going through and when you make it through, you should appreciate His Goodness. God is faithful, good, and sovereign. Faith is the master key that opens the door to the desires of our hearts from God.

Spiritual Food for Thought: Are you going to lean on God's understanding or yours?

Scripture References

Sovereign- 1st Timothy 6:15
Trust- Philippians 4:19, Psalm 27:14, Psalm 56:3
Faith- Mark 11:24, Ephesians 3:16-17, 1st Corinthians 16:13

D A Y

15

Song: Alabaster Box
Topic: Renewal of a New Heart
Scripture: Ezekiel 36:26 NKJV

I will give you a new heart and put a new spirit within you;
I will take the heart of stone out of your flesh and give you a
heart of flesh.

Luke 7:37-38 NKJV

And, behold a woman in the city who was a sinner, when
she knew that Jesus sat at the table in the Pharisee's house,
brought alabaster flask of fragrant oil, and stood at His feet,
behind Him weeping; and she began to wash His feet with
her tears, and wiped them with the hair of her head; and she
kissed His feet and anointed them with the fragrant oil.

Going through the storms of life can be very challenging. My
mother was in some dark places in her life when my siblings
and I were young, but God allows us to experience some

things in our lives to the point where we made it through the storm by God's grace. Then He also wants us to be a blessing to someone through our testimony. When my mom was growing up she needed emotional support and also needed to feel loved. Yes, mom grew up in Church, believed and had faith, but she let flesh in the way. Later on in her life, she started hanging with the wrong people, had three failed marriages, and almost lost me and my two sisters. As my mother got tired of being in that dark place, Psalms 23 is the scripture that took her through the very hard times in her life and she surrender all to God. God delivered, transformed, and healed my mom. Alabaster Box is my mom's favorite worship song, it tells her story. When she was praying and seeking forgiveness and renewing her relationship with her Lord and Savior with her whole heart, He stepped in and delivered her. As she was in pain physically, emotionally, and spiritually God heard her cry. When she felt God wrap His loving arms around her, she started praising, worshipping, and giving God all the honor and Glory. God restored our relationship and blessed us with the fullness of my mom's love, happiness, peace, trust, and joy. She is a living testimony of what God can and will do, just put your faith, hope, and trust in Him.

Spiritual Food for Thought: If He can and did do it for me, He can and will do it for you. "Unconditional Love"

Scripture References

Surrender – James 4:7, Romans 12:1-2, James 4:10
Delivered – Psalm 56:13, Romans 7:6, Psalm 32:7
Restore – Psalm 51:10-12, Joel 2:25, 1ˢᵗ Peter 5:10

D A Y

16

Song: Great is the Lord Thy Conqueror
Topic: Romans 8:37 NKJV
Scripture: God's Eternal Love

Yet in all these things we are more than conquerors through Him who loved us.

Great is the Lord thy conqueror, He has never failed me yet, through all my trials and tribulations. He will deliver. Because God is your Redeemer, Savior, Protector, Healer He's the Greatest, Great is the Lord. If you trust God nothing is impossible. It may seem that God has failed us, but He never fails. Think back over all the trials and tribulations God has brought you through. It may not come when you wanted, but, it was always on time in God's perfect plan and His will. Yet in all these things, we are more than conquerors through Christ Jesus who loves us. God answers our prayers and sees us through every situation according to His Sovereign will. God's Sovereignty is that there isn't anything that will enter your life that God does not either ordain or allow. He has authority over every situation in our lives. Because God never lies or fails, He keeps His promises, He will see you through your darkest moments. We must believe with the expectation that God responds when we diligently seek Him. Your greatest lessons in faith are often learned in the darkest moments of your life. This builds your character and faith.

Spiritual Food for Thought: Remember Great is the Lord thy Conqueror! When you pray ask God in His will and not ours.

Scripture References

Conqueror- Romans 8:35-37, 1st Corinthians 15:57, Hebrews 11:6
Trust- Philippians 4:19, 1st John 5:14, Jeremiah 17:7-8
Redeemer- Proverbs 23:11, Job19:25, Zephaniah 3:17

D A Y

17

Song: Speak to My Heart Holy Spirit
Topic: A Prayer of Restoration
Scripture: Psalm 51:10 NKJV

Create in me a clean heart, O God, and renew a steadfast spirit within me.

When we make a prayer of repentance of whatever we've done in our life, we need to consider two things, we need to ask God to renew a steadfast spirit within us and then ask God to create in us a clean heart so that we may serve Him. Just as David was asking that his heart be renewed, restored and transformed. God is the only source and has the power of such a renewal. Speak to my heart Lord. Give me your Holy Word. By receiving God's word we have to read, meditate, and imbibe the Scriptures in our hearts. You will receive God's word of love, and guidance as He is renewing, restoring, and transforming your heart. Lord, I want to be a worthy vessel as your Spirit guides and abides in me. For us to be a vessel, we are called unto honor by God's grace. That's

why any person can be used by God. We must be sancti-
fied and filled with the power of the Holy Spirit. Holiness
and Purification must be your lifestyle. There are several
principles of becoming a vessel unto honor. Be born again,
Stay away from sin, activate the fruit of the Spirit, and Set
your heart on the things of God. The fruits of the Spirit in
Galatians 5:22 (NKJV) are love, peace, longsuffering, kindness, goodness, faithfulness, gentleness, and self-control.

Spiritual food for thought: Do you need God to create in
you a Clean Heart so that you can be a Worthy Vessel?

Scripture References

Worthy Vessel- 2nd Timothy 2:21, Romans 9:21-23,
Holy Spirit- Romans 5:5, Romans 15:15-16, 1st Corinthians
6:19-20
Sanctified- Jeremiah 1:5, Hebrews 2:11, 2nd Timothy 2-21

DAY
18

Song: I Just Want to Praise You Forever
Topic: Praising the Lord for His Goodness
Scripture: Psalms 145: 1-2 Amp

I will exalt you my God, O King, and [with gratitude and submissive wonder] I will bless your name forever and ever.

Every day I will bless you and lovingly praise You; Yes, [with awe-inspired reverence] I will praise Your name forever and ever.

Lord, I just want to thank You and give You Glory, Honor, and Praise because You are so worthy to be praised. As we look at our lives and think of Your Goodness, Faithfulness, and Forgiveness, we should be in awe and reverence to you. Blessings and Glory and Honor, they all belong to You, Thank you Jesus for Blessing me. Everything belongs to you. We should Bless You and Praise You Forever. As we continue to walk in Your Blessings, we walk by faith and not just talk by faith. We have to have action in our faith walk, that is, whatever may come our way that's not of you, we know in our hearts that you got us. In your word, you said that you will never leave us or forsake us (Hebrews 13:5). Lord, I can't thank you enough for everything you've done for me. Our hearts should be filled with Gratitude no matter what life brings us. We should Praise God during the good times as well as the bad times, this builds our character, faith, and strength when the storms of life occur. This pleases God as we continue to Praise and Worship Him.

Spiritual food for thought: What will you do? Will you continue to Praise God Forever and how would You Praise Him?

Scripture References

Praise- 2nd Chronicles 20:21, Psalm 106:1
Exalt- Isaiah 25:1, Psalm 34:3
Blessing- Nehemiah 9:5, [Bless] Psalm 34:1, Jeremiah 29:11

D A Y

19

Song: He's Preparing Me
Topic: Putting on the Full Armor of God
Scripture: Ephesians 6:10-11 CSB

Finally, be strengthened by the Lord and by His vast strength. Put on the Full Armor of God so that you can stand against the schemes of the devil.

Because God cares for you, He's preparing you for something you cannot handle right now. He is maturing and arranging you and pruning you. God is Preparing You and providing you with what you will need for the Spiritual battle and various battles that will occur in your life. Remember the battle is not yours, it's the Lord. God is training us to hear His sweet voice and to put our total trust in Him. Sometimes the problem we are dealing with isn't of human origin. Yes, it's foolish to blame everything on the devil, but it's even more foolish not to recognize that he is at work. In Ephesians, Paul writes put on the whole Armor of God, so that we can stand against the devil's schemes. For our struggle is not against flesh and blood, but against the powers of this dark world and spiritual forces of evil in the heavenly realms. So we must put on the Full Armor of God every day, the Helmet of Salvation; the Breastplate of Righteousness; the Girdle of Truth; Sandals of Peace; the Shield of Faith which protects (guards) us from all fiery darts of the enemy; and we pick up the Sword of the Spirit, the Word of God. When you know the Word of God, you can speak the Word when facing trials, tests, tribulations, and temptations to cut to pieces the snare of the enemy. Thank you Lord for the Armor and thank You for preparing me for the Battle.

Spiritual food for thought: Are you going to fight your battle on your own, or are you going to put on the Full Armor of God?

Scripture References

Armor- Ephesians 6:10-18, Isaiah 59:17, 2nd Corinthians 10:5
Evil- John 17:15, Matthew 6:13, Psalm 23:4
Word- Proverbs 30:5, Psalm 119:105, Hebrews 4:12

D A Y

20

Song: Jesus you are The Center of My Joy
Topic: God's Love and Joy
Scripture: John 15:11 NKJV

These things I have spoken to you, that my joy may remain in you, and that your joy may be full.

John 15:11 describes a believer's experience of Christ's love and complete joy. There is a difference between happiness and joy. Happiness sometimes comes from external circumstances, it can be for a brief moment of spending time with family. Joy is internal because we have a firm foundation of our intimacy with Christ. Nehemiah 8:10 says, Do not sorrow, for the joy of the Lord is your strength. The joy of the Lord is the joy that springs up in our hearts because of our relationship with the Lord. It is a God-given gladness found when we are in communion with God. Remember, when it seems you are losing your Joy think of God's love, and hope for tomorrow. Joy is internal when you have the love, peace, and trust in the Lord. Trust in the Lord, He will give you joy and His joy will give you strength. I love to hear Shirley Caesar sing this old spiritual song, "this joy that I have, the world didn't give it to me and the world can't take it away." Call on Jesus, nobody but, Jesus. When you think of the goodness of God. He will bless you with unspeakable joy.

Spiritual food for thought: Strive to have internal joy and peace in your heart.

Scripture References

Joy – Galatians 5:22-23, Psalm 16:11, John 15:9-11
Happiness- Psalm 16:9, Psalm 37:4, Philippians 4:4
Hope- Romans 15:13, Psalm 130:5, Psalm 42:11

D A Y

21

Song: Oh Taste and See that The Lord is good
Topic: The Contentment of Those Who Trust in God
Scripture: Psalm 34:8 NKJV

Oh taste and see that the Lord is good; blessed is the man who trusts in Him!

Taste and see that the Lord is good. The taste of His goodness just speaks of the continuation of His Blessings. His Blessings, Grace, and Mercies are new every day. God is good at all times. Magnify the Lord and Glorify the Lord with me and let us exalt His name forever. When we think of His goodness, our cup overflows from the promises of God. A few of His promises are love, joy, peace, protection, provision, healing, eternal life, faithfulness, wisdom, salvation, confidence, help, and guidance. When storms of life hit you just think of His goodness. God will not fail you, have Faith, trust in Him and think of His promises. He'll give you everything. When God gives you Joy it's an unspeakable joy (inexpressible). 1ˢᵗ Peter 1:8-9 NKJV "Though now you don't see

Him, yet believing, you rejoice with joy inexpressible and full of glory, receiving the end of your faith the salvation of your souls." In knowing God and knowing of the overflow of His love, we have so much peace inward that no matter the situation we may be in, He will always be present with us. We serve and believe in an Awesome God that is the same yesterday, today, and forever. He never changes and His words are true according to His richness and glory.

Spiritual food for thought: Just sit back and meditate on God's Goodness.

Scripture References

Trust- 2nd Samuel 22:3, Psalm 37:3, Isaiah 43:2,
Goodness- Psalm 31:19, Psalm 52:1, Galatians 5:22-23
Promises- 2nd Corinthians 1:20, Hebrews 11:13, Hebrews 10:23

D A Y

22

Song: Change Me
Topic: Praying for Repentance
Scripture: Psalm51:10 NKJV

Create in me a clean heart, O God, and renew a steadfast spirit within me.

On January 14, 2020, I wrote in my journal that Change is about to come over me. I'm so glad He's changing me. Change is frightening, it could include numerous things that will make you feel like you've been stuck in situations that you know are not right with God. You want to do better, you want to have a clean heart, you want to move closer to God and have that spiritual intimacy with Him. In this song, it says, "Change me Oh God. Wash me through and through. Create in me a clean heart so that I may worship you. I need you to change me, only you can do it for me, Lord. Whatever I'm lacking from the inside out, Lord I need you to change me." In Psalm 51:10, David was asking that his heart be renewed, restored, and transformed. God will do the same for you. God is the only source of renewal. No matter what the change is, God goes before you preparing the way. Have confidence that through this change God will be there. Bring me peace in the midst of this change, so that I may not fear what is to come. Lord, I don't know what the future holds but, I Know Who Holds Tomorrow. Tell Jesus you trust Him with all your tomorrows and that you know He will be with you always. You said God in your word, that you will never leave me or forsake (abandon) me. As I will be obedient and walk closer with you, my faith will be strengthened. Oh, What a Wonderful change has come over me.

Spiritual food for thought: If you let Him. God can change you.

Heart- Psalms 139:23-24, Ezekiel 18:31, Jeremiah 17:9-10
Renewed- 2nd Corinthians 4:16, Ephesians 4:23-24, Colossians 3:10
Transformed- Romans 12:2, 2nd Corinthians 3:18,

D A Y
23

Song: Praying and Believing
Topic: Exhortations
Scripture: 1ˢᵗ Thessalonians 5:16-18

Rejoice always, pray without ceasing, and in everything give thanks; for this is the will of God in Christ Jesus for you.

As we hold fast to God's unchanging hands. Knowing without a doubt that He hears us. Praying will clear our vision to start seeing through God's eyes. Philippians 4:6-7 Amplified Bible says, "do not be anxious or worried about anything, but in everything [every circumstance and situation] by prayer and petition with thanksgiving, continue to make your [specific] requests known to God." Praying does work if we just Stand firm, Believe and trust God's Divine word. Continue to Believe and have Faith and not unwavering Faith in God. God said that we should cast all of our burdens unto Him and leave them there. He will and can handle anything, nothing is too hard or impossible for God. As we get older, our prayer life ought to be changing, we should be more obedient, depending on and totally trusting God in everything. Prayer makes you wait, Isaiah 40:31 NKJV says, "but those who wait upon the Lord shall renew their strength." And as we are waiting on the Lord for the deliverance of the prayers that we petition before Him. We should be still to hear God's voice for what He has for us through the Holy Spirit. He will give us peace in every situation we encounter.

Spiritual food for thought: Let go, Let God, Get out of His way, and watch Him work. Because when you've done all you can, just stand, He's working it out for you.

Scripture References

Stand- Ephesians 6:13, Ephesians 6:14, 1ˢᵗ Corinthians 6:13
Wait- Psalm 40:1, Isaiah 8:17, Psalm 27:14
Praying- Ephesians 6:18, Acts 16:25, Mark 11:24

D A Y

24

Song: In Times like These
Topic: God's Timing
Scripture: Ecclesiastes 3:1 NKJV

To everything there is a season, a time for every purpose under heaven.

In the NKJV, this poem speaks with eloquence about the role of time in the life of the believer. This poem speaks of the life that is lived in a relationship with God. Everything happens in God's appointed timing and His perfect Will. I have two dear friends, we call each other sisters, in 2019 they lost both of their parents in a month unexpectedly. Life is so precious, we are to cherish it and thank God each day for the breath He gives us. And as I spoke at their dad's home-going service, I told them, "as you think about the precious moments you had with your dad and little things will come to your remembrance, just start Praising God in everything. Henrietta's service was beautiful, you could feel the love in the room and her home-going service exemplified the life that she lived.

She loved the Lord. As we are Praising God through the process of our healing, God is receiving all the Glory. No matter what happens in life, God always promises to comfort us. He gives us comfort through His Holy Spirit. None of us are exempted from trials, tribulations, or grief. Comforting us directly, sometimes through circumstances and sometimes through the people He places in our lives. Nothing speaks more powerfully of your walk with God other than having a continuous Praise and thankfulness in your heart.

Spiritual Food for thought: Remember, the gift from God is life.

Scripture References

Comfort- Psalm 23:4, Matthew 5:4, 1st Thessalonians 4:18
Holy Spirit- John 14:16-17, Psalm 14:26-27, Romans 5:5
Glory- 1st Chronicles 16:10-12, Psalm 24:8-10, Psalm 145:10-11

Song: Praise Him
Topic: "Praise Ye the Lord"
Scripture: Psalm 150:6 NKJV

Let everything that has breath praise the Lord. Praise the LORD!

In God's word, it says, "let everything that has Breath Praise the Lord." God is worthy of every praise that we can offer to Him. There is none like Him, no not one. In the song 'Every Praise.' It says, "every Praise is to our God, Every word of worship with one accord. Every praise, every praise, every praise is to our God. Sing hallelujah to our God." Hallelujah is a declaration of praise or worship of God. It is the highest praise giving honor and reverence to God. God blessed us in so many ways so we ought to praise Him. Psalms 150:1 NKJV the Psalmist gives a call for Praise to God in His sanctuary. We can Praise God through song, dance, musical instruments, and prayer. As we praise God through singing, we are using the voice that God has blessed us with. We can praise and worship God through dance, just as David danced before the Lord with all his might. 2nd Samuel 6:14. We can praise God with musical instruments such as sounds of the trumpet, flute and harp, string instruments, and clashing cymbals. And praising God through prayer is an open line of communication with Him. Then, as we render praise to God it ends with a call to worship. Giving our full attention to admiring God for who He is and appreciating what He does. With deep love and reverence to God; giving our greatest praise to Him alone.

Spiritual Food for Thought: How would you Praise God?

Scripture References

Praise – Psalm 118:28-29, Psalm 145:3-7, Psalm 150:6
Prayer- Philippians 4:6-7, Ezra 3:11, Jeremiah 29:12
Worship- John 4:24, 1st Chronicles 16:9-12, Psalm 95:6-7
Reverence 1st Samuel 12:14, 1st Samuel 12:24, Psalm 111:10

D A Y

26

Song: I Need You Now
Topic: Prayers for Guidance
Scripture: Psalm 5:1-3 NKJV

Give ear to my words, O Lord, Consider my meditation.

2- Give heed to the voice of my cry, My King and my God, for to you I will pray. My voice you shall hear in the morning, O LORD; In the morning I will direct it to you, and I will look up.

This is a testimony of a young man who is 24 years old. He has been suffering from seizures, all his life. He is a strong person of faith. In January 2021, he decided to have brain surgery to alleviate the seizures. The surgery was successful, but while in the hospital, Cov-19 invaded his body. But, through this trial, he witnessed and testified that he knew God for himself. 1st John 2:3 NKJV says, "now by this we know that we know Him, if we keep His commandments." This simply means that one who has trusted Christ knows

Him (John 17:3) that is to say, has met Him. And one who has previously met the Lord can also come to know Him intimately (Phil.3:10) through his testimony. Kyle said that God choose him so he can have a closer and personal relationship with Him. He was testifying of the goodness of God of how he was healed from Cov-19 and how his surgery was a success. During this trial, what made him stronger was the awareness that God was with him all the time. The song, "I Need You Now" touched Kyle's heart and spirit as he was going through these trying times. The song says, "I stretched my hands to thee. Come rescue me, I need you right away. Not a second or another minute, not an hour or another day. But at this moment with my arms outstretched, I need you to make a way. I need You now Lord." Kyle felt God's gentle hug and loving arms around him as he was praising God. Deuteronomy 10:6, 8 says, "Be strong and of good courage, do not fear nor be afraid of them; for the Lord your God, He is the One who goes with you. He will not leave you nor forsake you." As you walk in your faith day by day, as He is elevating you to a new level in your life, God gives you endurance and wisdom. This young man stated that in the midst of recovering from his brain surgery and covid, he still had a reason to rejoice because God healed him and allowed him to be a witness to share his testimony.

Spiritual food for thought: Are you going to share your testimony?

Scripture References

Rejoice- Psalm 33:1, Philippians 4:4, 1ˢᵗ Thessalonians 5:16
Testifying- 1 Peter 5:12, Hebrew 11:4,
Wisdom- Ecclesiastes 3:26, Job 28:12,28, Proverbs 2:6

D A Y

27

Song: Your Steps are Order
Topic: God's Guidance
Scripture: Proverbs 16:9 NKJV

A man's heart plans his way, But the Lord directs his steps.

Sometimes in life, we procrastinate. We have a desire to start something but it just seems like we can't get started. We let distractions get in our way and deter us. In a message that was spoken by Pastor San Lee, it was so profound. She said what are you doing just standing there? What are you waiting for? God? We have to take the initiative to take the first step. Because He's waiting on you to take that step. You can't take that step without picking up your foot. Do it with the intention of moving forward. That means you must put your foot down sometime, so let it be a step toward your goal, your dream, or your vision. When will you take that first step? Tomorrow or next week? No, take a step today. That way you're no longer just standing still, you're heading somewhere. This is all about Faith and Obedience… totally depending on God to direct your steps.

Spiritual food for thought: Remember to let God order your steps. He never fails.

Scripture References

Steps- Psalm 119:133, Jeremiah 10:23, Proverbs 16:9
Ordered – Psalms 37:23-24, Psalm 121:3,
Direct- Proverbs 3:6, 2nd Thessalonians 3:5

D A Y
28

Song: I Almost Let Go
Topic: This is my Exodus
Scripture: Isaiah 41:10 NKJV

Fear not, for I am with you; be not dismayed, for I am your God. I will strengthen you, Yes, I will help you, I will uphold you with my righteous right hand.

This testimony was shared with me. I was going through a storm and at the lowest point in my life. I had resigned from a job of 16 years to focus on my business full time. Everything was going well, I was making a lot of money daily and then it happened. I allowed the flesh to overcome that gift that God has given me and my family. You know, in other words, I got selfish. See, when you are into self, you no longer think of others but you. I was making good money as an investor, doing whatever I wanted to do, and going to places some people just dreamt of going. I got to a point in my life that made me feel that I have accomplished this all by myself. It became all about me and no one else. You see, we serve a jealous God, there is no other but Him. I started idealizing the money and not giving God thanks for His blessings. God had to remind me that everything belongs to Him and not myself. God had broken me down for two years and I could not find a job or work anywhere. I almost lost my family and everything we own because of my selfishness. Money can't buy you salvation nor can it redeem you. I didn't know I was falling into the abyss of the world until God stepped in and saved me. In the book of Matthew 14:26-31, the disciples saw Jesus walking on the sea and were troubled, saying it was a ghost. And Jesus answered immediately saying, "Be of good cheer! It is I don't be afraid." Then Peter answered Him and said, "Lord if it is you, command me to come to you on the water." As Peter began to walk toward Jesus, he realizes that he was walking upon water and began to take his eyes off of Jesus. In other words, when I took my mind off of my Lord and Savior Jesus Christ, just as Peter began to fall, I also fell and began to sink. See, I felt like I had no reason to live anymore but I am so glad that my God stretched his hands out and saved me.

When we began to put ourselves first, it becomes an act of yielding to the flesh. Paul said in Romans 7:14-23 NKJV, "when I sought to do right, wrong was always present." In other words, when we yield to the desire or lust of the flesh, we fall into the Sins of the world which causes us to be separated from God. Do you know that God has a plan for you? I cried out to the Lord and He saved me! Two weeks later, God blessed me with a job to provide for my family. See, I know without a doubt, that He can and He shall supply you with all your needs.

Anonymous

Spiritual food for thought: Don't allow the flesh to delay your Blessings.

Scripture References

Saved- Acts 16:30-31, Ephesians 2:8-9,
Flesh- Mark 14:38, Romans 8:1, Galatians 5:16-17
Salvation- Romans 10: 9-10, 2nd Corinthians 5:21, Acts 4:12
Redeem- Galatians 2:20, Psalm 107:2, Psalm 103:4

D A Y

29

Song: Give me a Clean Heart
Topic: Praying for Repentance
Scripture: Psalm 51:10 NKJV

Create in me a clean heart, O God, and renew a steadfast spirit within me.

Have you been in a situation or have you been troubled about someone or something that made it hard for you to forgive? Yes, I have. I learned that forgiving someone is not about them, it's about you. "For if you forgive men their trespasses, your heavenly Father will also forgive you" (Matthew 6:14). We can accomplish forgiveness through the power of the Holy Spirit in us. Forgiveness gives you power, unforgiveness steals your power. What I mean about that is, don't give anyone the power to get you physically, mentally, emotionally disturbed, or discombobulated. Pray sincerely to God to help you to release those hurts, deep scars, and grudge against someone. An Unforgiven heart and bitter Spirit cause bitterness. Jesus knows your hurts and wounds. "Forgive and be forgiven" (Luke 6:37). "If you don't forgive, neither your Father in heaven forgive your trespasses" (Mark 11:25). Ask God that your heart be renewed, restored, and transformed. God is the only source of renewal. After that, thank God for the Spirit to forgive. Don't miss out on your Blessings of Forgiveness. You will have so much peace in your heart and spirit.

Spiritual Food for Thought: Who do you have to forgive today?

Scripture References

Forgiveness – Ephesians 4:32, Mark 11:25 Psalm 86:5
Spirit- Proverbs 21:27, Psalm 51:11, Psalm 31:5
Heart- Psalm 139:23-24, Colossians 3:12-13, Psalm 51:10

D A Y

30

Song: Blessed Assurance
Topic: Faith Unwavering Faith
Scripture: Hebrews 10:23 NKJV

Let us hold fast the confession of our hope without wavering,
For He who promised is faithful.

Blessed Assurance is a Christian hymn, a song of faith that
declares the faith we have in God. The lyrics of the hymn are
about the love and assurance we have in Jesus the Savior. As
I think back to when I was a little girl, sitting on the side of
my grandmother, watching her play the organ while singing
"Blessed Assurance Jesus is mine," I didn't know what those
words meant then, but I fully understand now. I've never
seen her faith waver. She had the Assurance, that certainty,
and self-confidence in her faith in Jesus. Have the faith in
God and approach Him confidently in prayer 1ˢᵗ John 5:14-
15. The book of John says that we must ask according to His
will in prayer. God's word is the core and solid foundation
for us to stand on. Without that foundation, we are not able

to grow in our faith daily. For we walk by faith and not by sight 2ⁿᵈ Corinthians 5:7. Don't lose heart have the faith and strength to keep standing no matter what challenges you are facing. Prayer does not cause faith to work, but Faith causes prayer to work. In Mark 5:25-34, the woman with the issue of blood had unwavering faith, she believed that if she could make it through the crowd to just touch the hem of His garment she will be healed of her affliction. With that faith, she touched Him and she was healed. But it was Him who is Jesus that healed the woman and not the hem of His garment. Now, as an adult, I have the Assurance of God that He is my Rock and Salvation. Also, we get to have a "foretaste of glory divine," the confidence in knowing that there is something better when we leave this world. That God has prepared a place for us after this life has passed. And that's eternity with Him. He will never leave you are forsake you. God is a healer, He's a provider, He's your anchor in the midst of a storm and God is the Author and Finisher of our faith.

Spiritual Food for Thought: When facing life challenges, will you continue to have Unwavering Faith?

Scripture References

Assurance – Hebrews 10:22, Deuteronomy 1:21, Hebrews 11:1
Faith- 1ˢᵗ Peter 5:9, Matthew 21:22, Hebrews 11:6
Foundation- 2ⁿᵈ Timothy 2:19, Proverbs 10:5, 1ˢᵗ Corinthians 3:11

D A Y

31

Song: God's Grace
Topic: God's Grace is Sufficient
Scripture: 2nd Corinthians 12:9 - 10

And He said to me, "My grace is sufficient for you, for My strength is made perfect in weakness."

How did I make it, all these years? How did I make it through the storms of life? I know it had to be you, God. It was God's Grace. I made it this far by the Grace of God. His Amazing Grace. I was sick as a child, I had open heart surgery at seven, bone disorder in my left leg, going through my pregnancy and delivery, I almost died. I delivered my beautiful baby girl on a Sunday by emergency c-section. I was in a coma and didn't get to see my daughter until that following Thursday. Went through a broken marriage. Years after that God blessed me with a God-fearing man, two daughters, and ten beautiful grandchildren. But by God's grace, He healed me physically, mentally, emotionally, and spiritually. Everyone has a story, by witnessing to others, that is your testimony. No one can tell your story like you can, because everyone's testimony is different. You see I know God is a God of Mercy, Deliverance, and Grace. When you didn't have any hope left, you thought God wasn't there for you. He's always with you. God said that He will never leave you nor forsake you (Deuteronomy 31:6-8). He said, trust in Me, don't look at your outward circumstances, look up to Me. From whence comes my help? (Psalm 121:1-4). His word never goes void. In this life you will have some storms that rage you, probably will be in one, going through one, or headed out of one. I'm here to tell you, that God will dry your tears Psalm 56: 9-11. It is by God's grace, His Amazing Grace for you to tell your story. He kept me and you here to be a witness to give your testimony. He delivered you by giving you the peace and reassurance of His love. We are still standing by the Grace of God. His Amazing Grace.

Spiritual Food for Thought – Will you be a witness to others and share your testimony?

Scripture References

Grace- Romans 6:14, 2nd Corinthians 12:9, Ephesians 2:8-9
Deliverance- Proverbs 21:31, Psalm 34:17, Psalm 34:4
Testimony- Psalm 78:5-6, Luke 21:13, John 8:14

9 7 9 8 9 8 6 3 8 2 9 0 6